Sue Parkinson

The Little Book of Happy

*By
Sue Parkinson*

MAPLE
PUBLISHERS

The Little Book of Happy

Author: Sue Parkinson

Copyright © Sue Parkinson (2025)

The right of Sue Parkinson to be identified as author of this work has been asserted by the author in accordance with section 77 and 78 of the Copyright, Designs and Patents Act 1988.

First Published in 2025

ISBN: 978-1-83538-801-3 (Paperback)
      978-1-83538-802-0 (E-Book)

Book Cover Design and Layout by:
　　Maple Publishers
　　www.maplepublishers.com

Published by:
　　Maple Publishers
　　Fairbourne Drive,
　　Atterbury,
　　Milton Keynes,
　　MK10 9RG, UK
　　www.maplepublishers.com

A CIP catalogue record for this title is available from the British Library. All rights reserved. No part of this book may be reproduced or translated by any form or by any means, electronic or mechanical, including photocopying, recording or by any information storage and retrieval system without written permission from the author.

The views expressed in this work are solely those of the author and do not reflect the opinions of Publishers, and the Publisher hereby disclaims any responsibility for them. This book should not be used as a substitute for the advice of a competent authority, admitted or authorized to advise on the subjects covered.

A

Absence makes the heart grow fonder.

When you're apart you realise how much you miss someone.

Value every second you're together.

Sue Parkinson

B

Believe in yourself, never give up on your dreams.

They may not all come true but that won't be for lack of trying!

C

Communication is the key!

Don't be afraid to start a conversation whether it be at the bus stop or the checkout, It's worth more face-to-face than all those online chats!

Sue Parkinson

D

Discover new horizons, every day your mind can explore as much as you allow it to!

Travel in the footsteps of others that have before.

E

Exercise your body and it will relax your mind, whether it be the gym, a walk, running or dancing!

This natural remedy will also release endorphins to the brain.

F

Friends are worth more than all the money in the world.

A good friend will be there for you during good and bad times.

Friends can be a natural support network.

Sue Parkinson

G

God will be there for you in any way, shape, or form.

You can talk to God about anything, and He will guide you.

God will never give up on you as long as you believe.

Sue Parkinson

H

Happiness is a gift we can all allow ourselves.

It will come in every way shape of form if we let it!

We can see it, feel, hear and touch it.

1

Instinct, the very base of what we think and feel, it comes from our heart.

Sometimes it warns us of danger, or it can tell us who we can trust!

J

Jealousy is a negative feeling.

It will never make us happy.

It just tells us what we think we want and can't have!

K

Kindness is a very positive attribute, it works both ways.

If we are kind to others, and they are kind to us there is an equal and rewarding balance!

L

Loss can cause many heartaches.

If we lose someone we love happiness then seems irretrievable!

Time is said to be the greatest healer Treasure the memories!

Sue Parkinson

M

Money, said to be the root of all evil, but can also bring great happiness to those who need it most!

They say giving is better than receiving.

Sue Parkinson

NEVER GIVE UP

N

Never give up on your dreams!

If they don't all come true, just treasure the memories of the ones that do! Never let dreams overtake reality!

O

Openness.

Open your heart and mind to everything and everyone around you.

By doing this we communicate and connect with the outside world!

Sue Parkinson

P

Patience. To many of us patience is our weakest virtue, waiting for someone or something.

Fill your mind with many different things, so as not to become impatient about one!

Sue Parkinson

Q

Questions. We continually question ourselves and others, to get the answers we feel we need, for our own peace of mind.

Answering questions can be fun! Quizzing can broaden our mind!

Sue Parkinson

R

Reliance. One way reliance can be a need, sometimes an addiction with an inanimate object Vapes, Cigarettes and Alcohol.

Self-reliance is a great inner strength!

S

Smile.

A smile is the visual way of showing how we feel. "I can be happy with life, happy to see you or even not happy and putting on a brave face!" It will usually bring a positive response.

T

Trust. Trust is a tricky one. Some say love many, trust few.

Others might say trust has to be earnt, and I believe that's true, we earn trust by being true to ourselves and others!

Sue Parkinson

U

Unexpected. Always expect the unexpected!

Without sounding obsessive always have a "In the event of" backup plan! Friends and family who turn up when you least expect them!

V

Valour. The dictionary describes valour as "bravery, courage and spirit"!

We can all embolden that power that helps us to overcome the dark times in our life!

Sue Parkinson

W

Warmth, is a good feeling. As opposed to a cold heart, warmth is a positive emotion that can spread to others. "Warm Welcome" is a phrase that has been in common use for many years.

X

Xmas, that time of the year that's "The Best of times and the worst of times!"

We want it all to be perfect, and we all try so hard! Sometimes you just have to chill out and have fun!

Sue Parkinson

Y

Yield! Always be open to others.

They may have different opinions,

but life's too short to argue!

By yielding, you are acknowledging their

right to theirs and yours.

Z

Zany, the ability to be zany, many interpret as "mad"!

Is it a bad thing sometimes when we look at life and everything that is happening in the world if we don't become this!

www.ingramcontent.com/pod-product-compliance
Lightning Source LLC
Chambersburg PA
CBRC091204070526
44584CB00007B/331